June. 1969

"The greatest of these is Love'.

I corinthians 13,

To you both with Love and Good.
Wishes

Mrs Fortin.

FORGET-ME-NOTS
OF LOVE

GOD'S PROMISES

POEMS AND LOVING
THOUGHTS
By Audrey McDaniel

FLORAL BOUQUETS
By Hazel Hoffman

He fashioned a flower
Of palest blue
A FORGET-ME-NOT
Of His Love
For you.

" . . . And where each Petal fell,
a PROMISE grew . . ."

"He gave us a Promise . . . . "

Who is your guest?
Hebrews 13:2

Be not forgetful to entertain strangers: for thereby some have entertained angels unawares.

BRING THE ROSES INDOORS:

Fill thy rooms with happiness. Carpet thy floor with roses that have been gathered in word or deed with dear ones. Add thy graciousness, thy mercy and thy concern for all who enter.

Encourage a prayer to bloom here reflecting, ". . . If ye have judged me to be faithful to the Lord, come into my house, and abide there . . ."
Acts 16:15

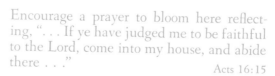

We ask for God to come to our door
And yet we forget the weary and poor
When we answer their knock upon our
   heart
God is our guest right from the start.

4

"He gave us a Promise . . . . ."

TWILIGHT:
Revelation 22:5

And there shall be no night there; and they
need no candle, neither light of the sun; for
the Lord God giveth them light: ...

REST WHEN EVENING FALLS:

The nocturnal King of Night lighted the
Heavens with His golden torch and Evening, as if loathe to leave the beautiful
scene, pulled her curtain down and pinned
it with a Star.

Close your eyes and put your heart at rest.
In order that the new day may be more
dedicated to God, ask thyself at daytime's
closing hour, "What have I done for Thee
this day?"

As I lay me down to sleep
Heavenly Angels guard may keep
God's Love the canopy o'er my head
Peace of soul shall blanket my bed.

5

"He gave us a Promise . . . . ."

A RAMBLING ROSE:
Mark 6:56

And whithersoever he entered, into villages,
or cities, or country, they laid the sick in
the streets, and besought him that they
might touch if it were but the border of his
garment: and as many as touched him were
made whole.

THE GREATEST LOVE STORY OF ALL:

Strolling through the New Testament with
that sweet Teacher of Galilee, we find Him
always busy about His Father's work. As
He talks with the Twelve, pearls drop from
His Lips; words of wisdom to be graven on
the hearts of men.

Footsore and weary going to the sick and
the needy, the just and the unworthy, min-
istering to all He met along the way.

Concluding His faithful service upon the
Cross that there might be HOPE and
ETERNAL LIFE for all He called His friends.

"He gave us a Promise . . . . ."

LOOKING ONE'S BEST FOR GOD:
Luke 12:27

Consider the lilies how they grow: they toil
not, they spin not; and yet I say unto you,
that Solomon in all his glory was not arrayed
like one of these.

WE CAN ALL BE BEAUTIFUL:

Regardless of our physical features, whether
homely or handicapped until only a soul
appears to remain, we can put on the rai-
ment of meekness, humility, tenderness and
then add affection, and as our countenances
radiate love we then begin to understand
what He meant when He said, ". . . in his
own image, . . ."   Genesis 1:27

Though we may not all be brilliant, our
hearts can be magnanimous in understanding. He gave all of us the potentials of
goodness. Our eyes may shine through a
make-up of patience, brotherly devotion
and happiness until we become truly beautiful.

7

"He gave us a Promise . . . . ."

GOD'S GARDEN:
Isaiah 51:3

. . . like the garden of the Lord; joy and gladness shall be found therein, thanksgiving, and the voice of melody.

THE MASTER ARTIST:

Lift up your heart. In every niche, your life has love tucked in.

God, in His infinite artistry, created a beautiful Dresden-like setting for you to find peace unto your soul; with His vast expanse of palest blue o'er head, the pink accent of fragrant blossoms and the white representing the purity of His Holy Example.

The whispered affection of a loved one, the soft note of a downy bluebird and the inspiration of a sacred hymn bespeak the beauty He designed to help you and to put your heart at rest.

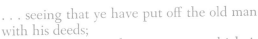

"He gave us a Promise . . . . ."

THE PRECIOUS GOLDEN YEARS:
Colossians 3:9, 10

. . . seeing that ye have put off the old man
with his deeds;
And have put on the new man, which is
renewed in knowledge after the image of
him that created him.

IN OUR BEAUTIFUL MEMORY:

Prettiness goes with youth, but beauty goes
with maturity. These years of experience
are rich in the knowledge of God's constant
Love, the happiness of friendships, a rainbow after a storm and the wisdom of a time
to sow and a time to reap.

How can a man be reborn when he is old?
— by letting the beautiful Love of God, that
cleanses and refreshes, re-enter his heart
until he is born anew.

Count your days by tender loved ones
Count your years with God so near
And with every added moment
Smile, because you serve Him here.

"He gave us a Promise . . . . ."

Reflecting faith:
1 Corinthians 13:13

But the Greatest of These is Love.

THE CLOVER TELLS A STORY:

In the creation of a tiny clover one finds a leaf for FAITH, one for HOPE and one for LOVE, and they are joined by a lone stem as a sort of parable of Jesus' Day, meaning all three of these blessings are within our very reach by a single grasp of the hand.

Then we find a dainty blossom reflecting a further lesson in the power of its Creator.

Consider it after a severe storm which moved the roof of a housetop; this dainty flower still standing on its frail stem erect to God.

"He gave us a Promise . . . . ."

KNOWING HIM, NOT JUST ABOUT HIM:
Psalms 46:10

Be still, and know that I am God: . . .

FROM TEARS TO SMILES:

There is a Divine Mission in every heart-break. The disappointments we experience only tend to turn us to God.

These sadnesses are only an interruption of our happiness that we may come to know Him, not just about Him, and then we will never want to leave Him realizing all of the hours He has faithfully gone through with us.

As the cares of life send us to Him, time and again, we learn there is no heartbreak His Love cannot heal.

"He gave us a Promise . . . . ."

To help us overcome illness:
James 5:15, 16

And the prayer of faith shall save the sick . . .
. . . and pray one for another, that ye may be healed . . .

HE MAKETH SOME OF US TO LIE DOWN TO UNDERSTAND AND SERVE:

In these shut-in hours we find the Divine Blessing of having time to meditate. Sometimes, these sick hours are the sweetest interludes we shall ever know with God.

If we pray BELIEVING and NOT WITH DOUBT IN OUR HEARTS, we can experience the true meaning of "HIS HEALING POWER" so that we can hold the hands of others in their restricted days.

12

PLEASE LORD JESUS

Cleanse me with Your Precious Blood
Heal me with Your Tender Love
Teach me this one thing to see
All of me belongs to Thee.

"He gave us a Promise . . . . ."

O ANGEL OF THE GARDEN:
1 Peter 1:24, 25

. . . The grass withereth, and the flower
thereof falleth away: But the word of the
Lord endureth for ever . . .

LIKE A ROSE:

This beautiful life likened unto the Rose
of Sharon. Rising early in the morning as
the Petals of a Rose unfurl, dew kissed by
God's Love — to sanctify another day — to
bring another life to happiness.

So blossomed this GREAT HEART for others
— permeating the fragrance of righteous-
ness — breathed into the hearts and souls
of men.

The Sacred Rose that softened a tear —
THE ONE ROSE.

THIS LOVE OF JESUS

In every prayer He made to heaven
He asked for LOVE for you
Sought HOPE to ease your every care
With faith and comfort new.

And when a cruel and empty tomb
Turned radiant with His Love
I knew He bought the things for you
That had been planned above.

That HOPE He left within your heart
To live your whole life through
O Saviour, Hope of all mankind
Our loving thanks to you.

"He gave us a Promise . . . . ."

EVERYTHING IS ANSWERED:
Mark 13:31

Heaven and earth shall pass away: but my words shall not pass away.

ONLY TRUST HIM:

God bestowed Jesus, His son, with the wisdom to give us an Eternal answer to everything.

Even though He was of divine wisdom, He left the answers in a simple — Theme of Love.

The things we could not quite comprehend, He taught us to trust God for — and strengthen Faith.

The Promises of God are guaranteed. We write defeat into our own script when we doubt. Christ taught us to pray believing.

"He gave us a Promise . . . . ."

PRAYER, LIKENED UNTO A WEAVER:
Romans 8:25

. . . then do we with patience wait . . .

AT THE LOOM:

Prayer is likened unto a weaver sitting at a loom. We pray for something very expedient in our lives or for some one we love.

Days pass — no change — the colors on the loom are drab and grey and no pattern is discernible.

Suddenly, we see our prayer unfolding. The PATTERN ON THE LOOM takes shape and form. Be patient — wait.

GOD IS THE WEAVER, He sits at the loom.

"He gave us a Promise . . . . ."

LOVE IS THE ANSWER:
1 John 4:8

. . . for God is love.

THE SECRET OF IT ALL:

If we would only fill the vacuum of our lives with love — love answers so completely — it would not matter, as we plow through this maze of existence, from whence we came or where we were going.

PERFECT LOVE CASTETH OUT FEAR. Any further transcending we might do would only be by way of love.

Love begets love. If we give love to others, it manifests itself to God and we receive a blessing.

Then LOVE IS EVERLASTING for . . . GOD IS LOVE.

"He gave us a Promise . . . . ."

PRAYING . . . HIS WAY:
James 5:16

. . . The effectual fervent prayer of a right-
eous man availeth much.

THIS PRAYER THAT PLEASES HIM:

We need not make arduous speeches, or
offer up impressive supplications.

In that moment of intimate affection, may
our very souls be permeated by the sanctity
of these sacred seconds.

With the latch open on the inside of our
hearts that God may enter, may we re-
veal deep humility, absolute confidence
and everlasting gratitude engrossed in love
worthy only unto Him.

"He gave us a Promise . . . . ."

WE NEED NEVER WALK ALONE:
Hebrews 13:5

. . . I will never leave thee, nor forsake thee.

SIDE BY SIDE:

He longs to:
be part of our plans and lead us in the way
everlasting — search our hearts and know
our thoughts — shelter and sanctify —
in this togetherness.

If we were absolutely alone in this life, His
Love could suffice to fill our every need as
He is the only ULTIMATE LOVE of perfect
balance.

He is our LOVING COMPANION and GUIDE
and will not forsake us on the way.

WHY ALL THE TEARS

God and I met
One sad and ill day
Burdened with problems
My eyes drooped to pray
Why all the tears
Don't you know you have Me
If you walk by My side
These things cannot be.

God and I met
On another day
Lifted in spirit
My soul longed to pray
Out of this love
The meetings grew
Don't walk wearily alone
God invites you too!

"He gave us a Promise . . . . ."

TO COMFORT YOU:
Revelation 7:17

. . . and God shall wipe away all tears from their eyes.

DON'T CRY . . . TELL GOD:

Remember the force of yesterdays' tears is not as strong as the Love of God which gives us the strength to start a new day.

He understands these tears. He gave His Only Son upon a cruel cross that we might have LOVE. He will not leave you comfortless now.

Through your sad loss others may see the lesson in Faith as you carry on in God's Name, not charging these heartbreaks up to Him.

He is PERFECT LOVE and real loves does not hurt us. He is standing by more tenderly than ever to help and He is the ONLY ONE that can put the sunshine back into our hearts.

WHERE LOVED ONES WAIT

Urns of roses dripping o'er
Primrose paths to make a floor
Love birds nestled in the trees
A sacred hymn to swell the breeze
Everywhere a pleasant word
Then God's precious Voice is heard
This the Mansion high above
Christ said God prepared with love
Here He teaches in this bower
How to make a tender flower
Tucks our Loved Ones down to rest
In this place that they love best
Dimly lights the Evening Star
Keeping watch where e'er they are
Let not tears make life seem o'er
Their Souls live forevermore.

"He gave us a Promise . . . . ."

THERE IS . . . HOPE:

When you come to the end of the rope —
tie a knot and hang on.

WHY NOT TRY GOD?

Your Heavenly Father knows you have
need of HOPE before you ask Him for something to motivate your life.

Too often, we toss ourselves to and fro in
this proving ground of living and employ
every means on earth to answer our needs,
SAVE GOD.

Of more value than RUBIES and PEARLS
are these reassuring words if we would only
look to God . . .

Hitherto have ye asked nothing in my
name: ask, and ye shall receive, that your
joy may be full.

John 16:24

24

"He gave us a Promise . . . . ."

IN TEMPTATION . . . WHERE IS GOD?
Job 5:19

. . . there shall no evil touch thee.

THIS IS GOD CALLING:

At the brink of temptation, lured by the
things we thought we wanted most . . . do
we encounter pain and anguish? Then God
was never more near. He is ever mindful of
our weaknesses and as evil o'er takes us He
draws closer . . . tenderly calling us through
the unrest back to His Side.

Only through faith and trust in Him can
we know His happiness and blessings.

Once you know His joy and peace then will
you find pardon, love and release.

25

"He gave us a Promise . . . . ."

SEARCHING FOR GOD:
Jeremiah 29:13

And ye shall seek me, and find me, when
ye shall search for me with all your heart.

James 4:8

Draw nigh to God, and he will draw nigh
to you . . .

STAY WITH GOD:

For it is written, ". . . he shall give his
angels charge over thee, to keep thee . . ."

Psalm 91:11

Then He perfumed these blossoms
With FAITH, HOPE and LOVE
And sprinkled them with blessings
For you from above.

FROM GOD WITH LOVE

A Rose in a garden
To soften a tear
A Loved One to whisper
That friendship is near
Prayers to caress you
Each step of the way
These are His Gifts
Which are with us to stay.

TAKE
EVERY
DREAM

Take every dream within your heart
To God who really cares
He longs to hold you in His Arms
He listens for your prayers

Take every sigh and every tear
To Him who understands
Exchange these things for lasting peace
Within His loving Hands.

SOMEWHERE ALONG THE WAY

When some sad heart I met today
Did I use prayer to show the way
When some weary soul sore oppressed
Needed love to find peace and rest
Was I the one to say the word
Or leave them hurt and unheard
Did I have courage down in my heart
Enough to give them a brand new start
Was there patience ample for two
Did I care as I ought to do
Or did I see them walk away
Without sharing His Love today.

BECAUSE
THY LOVE IS NEAR

I thank Thee Father for Thy Love
Revealed to me from Heaven above
In sounds of laughter, fragrant air
In all the comfort of Thy care
Let all the deeds my life may do
Be something God that pleases You.

SUNBEAMS

When my life seemed sad and grey
And I thought I'd lost my way
A beam of sunshine filled my room
There stood God amidst the gloom

He stretched out His Arms to me
Took my burden, set me free
Gave me love and joy too
There's enough for me and you

Stay with Him each dawning day
He will bless you as you pray
There'll be sunbeams in your heart
You'll know from Him you cannot part.

A LILY WHITE

As a Lily of the Easter theme
Tells of His Great Love Supreme
As Promise on a Cross was hung
That HOPE for you had just begun
Then do not feel that life's in vain
He bore the stripes to save us pain.

MY DEAREST LOVE

The hours I spend with Thee Dear God
Intrigued by love so true
The magic of the spell You weave
To keep me close to You

I find in Thee my Dearest Friend
A tender, gentle care
I could not make my way in life
Unless my plans You'd share

For Thou art all the things I need
The Love I seek in prayer
A rainbow's peaceful, Dresden hue
To tell me You are there.

DEAR GOD make me a symbol of Thy Holiness. Create within me an understanding heart. If some soul be seeking LOVE, let me reflect Thy Love through my affection.

PLEASE FATHER, help me not to be so concerned about myself, but about Thee. If there be those who are lonely, let me take the hands of these dear ones and turn their sadness into HOPE.

MAKE ME A FRIEND

My friends from God will always be
Like petals of a rose to me
Each heart a pearl, each one a prayer
Wafted on earth's fragrant air
I thank Thee God for them each day
I'll try to understand their way
Listen to their secrets too
And never tell a soul but You
More important than the rest
I would have them love Thee best.

GUIDANCE

My Father knows the way
I cannot see

Within His Hands

He has a Gift of Love
for me

So I will ever pray
with open plea

For He will know what
is the best for me

Not chain His Hands

Or ask for something
planned by me

But trust My Father

For the things I cannot see.

O ROSE STREWN WALL

Just beyond the garden wall
I can hear my Saviour call
There beside a pink rose tree
Loving Angels wait for me
A celestial organ plays
Prayers entwine my precious days
Take God's Hand and you will see
What He has in store for thee.

"He gave us a Promise . . . . ."

While we are absent, one
from the other:

God bless thee loved one as we part
Bow thy head with humble heart
Say a prayer to God for me
I will pray each day for thee.

I leave a rose within thy hand
God give thee friends to understand
For every Promise of His Love
May we give thanks to Him above.

Gather this bouquet
He left just for you
Of HIS TENDER LOVE *with*
FORGET-ME-NOTS *too*.